The Happy Woman

Hope,
Strength,
Love

The Happy Woman

Hope,
Strength,
Love

HANADI ALQATARI

First published in the United Kingdom in 2018 by
The Choir Press

ISBN 978-1-78963-007-7

Contents

∞ৎ৯∞

Introduction

∞⌇∞

In July 2015, I started writing my first words in my book, *The Happy Woman: Hope, Strength, Love.*

It was a proud moment. God has blessed me with a strength and purpose in this life. It's a great feeling to be a voice for the countless women – mothers, married, single, divorced, widowed, lovers etc. – who need the world to know, to understand the uniqueness, love, feeling, strength and energy of all of us out here making our way on our own.

I have encountered difficult times and happy, times of depression and times of failure, moments of success and satisfaction in my life, and inspiring words of wisdom have always made all the difference. Even if they are simple.

I have found that every woman among us needs motivational words, inspiring quotes or anything to believe in throughout the days.

This book is a collection of quotes, wise words and sayings which I believe in my own life, but remember that you do not have to believe in everything. You are the master of your way you live your life. You can make it what you want it to be.

Love first and last and you will find the right way.

Love you all.

Hanadi Alqatari

Hope

‘

You are a human. Bad choices do not mean you are bad.

HANADI ALQATARI

It is your choice to let your past experiences teach and empower you in your life.

When you make decisions you regret, it leads to stress that affects your future choices, even if the decisions you regret are small. Learn from those decisions, but put that regret behind you; never carry it forward into the future with you.

So much of our journey and life is about good and bad. Experiences are what keep us learning, exploring and growing. Remember that every choice you make, whether 'good' or 'bad', will lead you to a destination you were supposed to be at.

Sometimes you will have a difficult time making decisions, regret your choices or feel shame about an error you have made, but it is natural to feel that way and it is not just you. You just need to appreciate your mistakes and be grateful for your choices, because they are yours alone.

You have an inner light, which comes from within.

HANADI ALQATARI

All our struggles and hard times will conspire to dim the light within us over time. But, if we allow all of our hopes, dreams and visions to fill up our soul, the light will shine brightly. Our soul supports our life in finding whatever we need.

Your heart/soul connection is magical power that comes from your great inner strength, your ability to know who you are and your place in the universe. Open up your consciousness to come spiritually alive and raise your inner light to connect with your soul.

'*If you want to live a happy life, tie it to a goal, not to people or objects.*

ALBERT EINSTEIN

Ignore everybody and start following your dreams. Do not let other people's negativity stop you from achieving your goals. Following your goals and dreams will make you alive, attractive and an inspiration to others.

Stand up for the things you believe in.

There are no laws in life saying there are limits to achieving what you want.

Your dreams are only yours.

If someone wants you in their life, they'll make room for you. You should not have to fight for a spot. Never, ever insist yourself to someone who continuously overlooks your worth.

UNKNOWN

Life is too short to spend time with someone who sucks the happiness out of you. People will come in and out of your life, and not everyone will make you smile and feel good.

Do not wait. Do not hang around people who do not care. You should not be forced to always give more than you get. Just let them go.

Doing so does not mean you hate them. It means you respect yourself.

*Life is beautiful. Cut out
negativity, forget gossip, say
goodbye to people who hurt
you. Spend your days with the
people who are always there.*

UNKNOWN

Life is precious. You could spend your days thinking about things that you have no control over, worrying about what people say and what they think of you.

It is not easy to be optimistic every day of the year. These feelings are very natural.

Be in love with your life, in love with every minute of it, and surround yourself with true friends who will bring out your inner light. Focus only on what matters.

Once you open the blinds to these matters and start spending your days wisely, you will release yourself from stress and anxiety and will start following a road towards peace.

‘

Accept what is, let go of what was, and have faith in what will be.

Sometimes you just need to relax and have faith that you will be taken care of in this life. You cannot control everything, and if you concentrate only on what you do not have, you will never have enough.

You may have failed or not taken enough time for yourself in the past, but live life for yourself, accept what you have in your life with gratitude, do not judge yourself by your past, and everything else will fall into place. Have faith take care of what you want to be tomorrow.

'

The hardest walk is walking alone, but it also makes you stronger.

We fear being without anyone to hold our hand or without a shoulder to lean on. This is natural, and we often try to ignore this feeling or deny it.

This is one of the greatest causes of our stress.

I have learnt that walking alone is really hard and sometimes even painful, but it is worth it, and it will make you explore your own feelings and who you really are.

Walking alone is nothing to fear. You are strong enough to stand on your own two feet and take time for yourself.

Respect yourself and your privacy.

'What goes around comes around.

UNKNOWN

Spread the message of love and peace wherever you go, practise saying good words and keep your social circle positive by thinking of good thoughts.

Being able to show gratitude and to feel, give and receive love is a blessing, and many people are simply unable to do so. It is up to each and every one of us to take every day as a new opportunity to give as much as we need to receive. We will feel grateful for what we are able to give those around us.

This does not mean you ignore your own needs.

6

I fall,
I rise,
I make mistakes,
I live, I learn,
I have been hurt but I am alive.
I am human, I am not perfect,
but I am thankful.

UNKNOWN

Each and every one of us has our own flaws, but the cracks and flaws we each have make us who we are.

Every beauty and joy in your life comes from accepting all the pain and tough times in life and extracting the good from everything happening to you.

No matter how many times you fall, there will always be the opportunity to evolve into something better.

All you have to do is be faithful and keep trying to find what you have inside you that keeps you going and living.

'*Watch your words; they have great impact. Use them wisely.*

UNKNOWN

Recently I became conscious of the power of the daily words I use and how they affect other people. When I realised that words were so impactful I started to think about most of the words I said. They have tremendous power that will affect others, ideally in positive ways.

We all have challenges in life, and many of us frequently complain of the negativity of the news we hear. I am not suggesting that we deny reality, but we can choose what we talk about to change our words into a positive state.

We can positively impact the world and our personal health by the words that we speak.

'

Remember, as long as you are breathing, it is never too late to start a new beginning.

UNKNOWN

Life is constantly changing and we are changing with it. We are not the same person we were before. Change is what it is all about, and every ending is the beginning of something else. However you are feeling today, know that things will get better and today is a new beginning.

Do not hold yourself down by dwelling on the changes you cannot control. The best thing you can do is to let go of what you cannot control, live simply and accept what has passed.

Today is a new beginning and you are right here, right now, with what you have, breathing. You have the ability to rebuild yourself, stronger than ever before.

'

*You cannot control everything.
Sometimes you just need to
relax and have faith that things
will work out. Let go a little
and just let life happen.*

KODY KEPLINGER

Letting go does not mean you do not care about the world and its challenges. It is just realising that the only thing you truly have control over is what you do. Do what makes you happy, search for the glimmer of hope inside you, and the good things will follow.

It is hard to let go and relax, but you will recognise the value of it once you do, no matter what you are going through.

Never force things. Give it your best and everything will fall into place eventually. Until then, you must always have faith in what could be.

'

Be thankful for every moment of your life, no matter what it is, good or bad. Gratitude will light up your life and rekindle hope.

HANADI ALQATARI

We always focus our mental energy on what we lack, not what we have. This can lead to worry, anxiety and depression.

When you are feeling down and things are not going your way, remind yourself, what do you have to be grateful for? Find something to look forward to. Big or small, count your blessings. Find a way to be thankful for your troubles, and they can become your blessings as well.

This is the power of gratitude.

'

Be grateful for people who add joy to your life without even being around you all the time. Being appreciated is the simplest and most incredible feeling you can give them.

HANADI ALQATARI

Each of us has those people who are close to our heart and make us feel comfortable even just by remembering their love and companionship.

If you only focus on what is wrong with others, if you think of your ex-friends and how you feel they have wronged you rather than thinking of your friends now, you will not experience joy; you will experience depression and low self-esteem. Focus on those closest to your heart and your soul and on rebuilding those relationships to experience joy and happiness.

Think of ways you can tell those people what you really feel, love them through good and bad times and appreciate them in a way that will make them truly feel appreciated.

'

Aim to be so busy loving life, and work so hard to achieve your dream, that you have no time for drama, regret, hate or fear.

HANADI ALQATARI

Take your first big steps toward your dreams. There is no dream too big. Stop waiting for life to happen for you. Change your frame of mind from waiting to doing. The world is your oyster.

Whatever goals you are thinking of right now, make a point of paying attention every day to recognise all the things that will bring you closer to those goals. Just a little bit of focus and thought about what it is you really love doing in this life is worth taking to live drama-free.

Be thankful for your life, spend time in nature, breathe deeply, let go of your worries, forgive yourself and others, and build your life around what you love.

UNKNOWN

Most of us find that time goes quickly and we never stop or slow down. Whatever you do, whatever problems you have or goal you are rushing to get to, remember to smile every chance you get. Not because life has been easy, but to help you calm down and slow down to savour the little moments in your life.

Accept what life hands you. Busy routines are not good for your health or your stress levels.

When you start to take deep breaths and be kind to yourself in thoughts, words and actions, you are always free to do something that makes you love your life.

You deserve it.

In all the rush to be more and achieve more, do not forget to be happy and appreciative.

BRENDON BURCHARD

Think about where you are in your life today and allow yourself to feel happy about your blessings, rather than only thinking about your problems.

It is good to focus on what we want to achieve, but it is not enough just to do that. There is also something beautiful in choosing to be appreciative, to feel happy and bright.

'

You will get what you put into this life.

HANADI ALQATARI

In life, you get what you put in. Everything comes back around. And we must always be mindful and conscious of what we are telling ourselves; our beliefs have more power than what we dream or wish or hope for. You become what you believe.

Make sure you send positive thoughts to the universe, and good things will come back to help you pursue the dreams you believe in.

Take time, every day, to do what makes your soul smile.

UNKNOWN

If you feel your day started badly and you start to get down or frustrated, treat yourself the way you would treat a loved one who needs your love and care, and never lose an opportunity to see anything beautiful.

Sometimes you have to forget what you want and just think of what you need. Sleep in, meditate or exercise.

Do one thing for yourself every day and feel your soul light up with appreciation.

'It is your choice to feel blessed, to feel grateful, to be excited, to be thankful, to be happy.

HANADI ALQATARI

We all have full responsibility for our thoughts, our actions, and the results they produce. We are always in a state of creation; we always have been. We are creating our thoughts in every moment of every day, either consciously or subconsciously.

Most of us go through life just reacting automatically and unconsciously to the events that take place around us. Perhaps you are having a bad day or someone has treated you unfairly; maybe you will emotionally react in a negative way to these situations. If so, it might be a good time to learn to consciously respond in a different, more positive way and find out how to manage your thoughts and feelings.

'

Smile often, dream big, laugh freely. Any happiness you get, you have got to make yourself.

HANADI ALQATARI

Your feelings are part of your internal guidance system. However old you are, the thoughts you think, your feelings, the things you are focusing on are actively moving you in the direction of your dreams and happiness.

Never be ashamed to express and show your feelings because they are different, and never let anyone make you feel bad about how you are feeling.

You can live the life you imagine and you deserve all the happiness in the world. Do what makes you happy, and find a way to extract positivity and fuel your happiness.

Remind yourself that your positive feelings will create results you desire.

'

*True joy comes when you live
the life you have imagined.*

HANADI ALQATARI

Listen to your feelings and dreams, believe in them and you will
create the life of your dreams.

You cannot just sit back and wait for the joy to come to you. You are
more powerful than you realise. You can create so much in your life
when you start to do everything that you set your mind to.

Each day make sure you are living out the life you have imagined.
Imagination does not have to be delusion; it could be an open-
mindedness that allows us to see what could be. It allows us to be
free from the limiting reality we live in.

'

Happiness starts with you.
You have everything you
need inside you.

HANADI ALQATARI

D o not search outside yourself; do not count on others to cheer you up. Rely on yourself rather than on others to do what is best for you.

Each and every one of us has light inside us, and we just need to notice that inner light. We are truly powerful human beings.

Everything you need to be happy is within you. Be kinder and gentler with yourself; let your light shine instead of allowing negativity to fester. The more you look inside yourself, the more successful and happy you will be.

To find happiness within yourself, spend time in exploring yourself and the things that delight you. Add those things to your life.

When you have chosen to find happiness within yourself, you will enjoy your inner happiness at all times.

'*Keep smiling no matter what life throws at you. There is always light at the end of the tunnel.*

HANADI ALQATARI

Whatever you are dealing with, know that the pain always passes, and feeling good about yourself will help. I am not saying it is always easy, but it can become easier when you believe that when you go through hard times, the result will be good.

Remember, you cannot always control what happens to you, but you can control how you choose to respond.

'

Be happy in your pain, strong in your weaknesses. Do not let pain remove any and all joy from your life.

HANADI ALQATARI

When times are hard, keep looking for anything that might make you feel stronger and more able to access the deepest joy.

Get out, go places and do things. Try to find some times to give you a little joy and peace. Pain is still there, but remind yourself of how wonderful life is and that it is always darkest before the dawn.

'

When choosing to think about the past or the future, you cannot fully appreciate living in the moment.

HANADI ALQATARI

Think about how you are living completely free today. Make a decision to appreciate where you are now. Do not be too busy solving the past and worrying about the future.

There is a difference between thinking about great things that happened in the past and making yourself feel bad by thinking about what you did yesterday. And there is a difference between worrying about the future and setting goals or plans for the future.

Our world is changing so fast that you will find time goes quickly. If you do not stop worrying about tomorrow and living in the past, it will take the joy out of living today.

'

Give voice to your dreams.
If you do not talk about
them, you will not
achieve them.

BRENDON BURCHARD

D o you have a dream or goal you are really working hard to achieve, or that you don't know how to begin working towards? First of all, remove the distance between yourself and your dreams by giving them a voice.

You need courage to talk about what you want. Do not be ashamed of your dreams or ashamed of planning something.

Having the courage to talk about your deepest dreams will give you excitement every time you think about them.

You have this voice within you. Start to talk about your dreams now to move yourself closer to what you want.

> *Life is short. Do not take everything so seriously. Be the one who brings joy and happiness.*

HANADI ALQATARI

There are times when we take ourselves a bit too seriously. These times cause us stress and make us think that the weight of the world is on our shoulders.

We are all going to do some pretty stupid and embarrassing things in our lives. If we can laugh at ourselves before people laugh at us, then we can magically make ourselves cheerful through the power of happy feelings.

You can be a hard worker without being serious all the time.

Work hard and enjoy hard. There is a link between being motivated to succeed at work and being motivated to find joy.

'

Do not live in fear of what may never happen.

HANADI ALQATARI

Worry is a circle round and round in your head; it is a fear of the unknown. Worry is a behaviour that does not do anything but stress us out.

Whenever you are feeling worry about an unresolved issue, it is best to make a decision to be aware of your thoughts and find your own way out of that negative feeling.

Sometimes, when your worries are holding you back from achieving something, clear your mind and ask yourself, 'What is the worst thing that could happen?'

Try to let go of the fears and take a bold step toward the unknown. Trust that you really do have the power to take care of what will happen.

Beat the fear. You are not powerless.

> *Sit down. Relax by doing something you enjoy. It really works out only when you have 'me time'.*

HANADI ALQATARI

Taking care of yourself does not have to be complicated; it does need to be fun, inspiring, nurturing. Sort out what you think you need from what you actually need.

When you do loving things for yourself, you quite naturally take yourself into a whole new space and time. Taking care of yourself is a force of energy that enables you to give your truest to create your life as you want it to be. There are countless wonderful ways to take time off to refresh your soul.

Even if you are stressed out struggling with a heavy workload, beat that stress by valuing and making space for your 'me time'. Do not finish your life with the regret that you were so busy working that you did not have enough time for yourself.

'Me time' is not a luxury. It is all about maintaining a good sense of self, and you should not feel guilty about it.

> ‘

Whatever your age, new beginnings are possible.

HANADI ALQATARI

I try to discover another way to live every day. Every day is a new beginning. When you are deeply unhappy, why not try new things?

You are free to move on, to break out of routines and comfort zones. As long as you are breathing you are able to try new things. Life at any age can be an adventure and full of memorable moments.

When you have settled into a routine and you feel that it is hard to get out of, remember you are not stuck permanently. Whatever your age, just be ready to try something new.

When you realise it is never too late to do what you want, I guarantee that you will make the best out of your life.

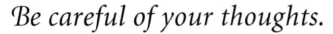

Be careful of your thoughts.

HANADI ALQATARI

Pay close attention to the power of thought. It is a creative power. The thoughts that pass through our minds have a powerful effect on our lives, for good or bad. When you believe something is good for you, this mighty power helps it to become so.

Once you listen to your thoughts, your thoughts will hold the power to create your reality.

Be assured that your positive, strong thoughts can create the reality of massive success in your life.

'

Nothing is impossible. There is a light at the end of the tunnel.

HANADI ALQATARI

When you are able to focus on a goal, your dreams will come true.

If you want to follow your dreams, do not sit back and wait for a miracle to happen. Take a moment to write down your top-priority goals and focus on those goals as much as you can.

It is time to start today. No matter what you fear others might expect of you, you will not allow this to stop you.

Work hard, dream big and make your dreams happen. One day you will become an inspiration to those around you.

> *Live your life without regrets.*
> *Forgive yourself and move on.*

HANADI ALQATARI

You can't change what has already happened. Be thankful for what you have now. Enjoy the journey of life; don't just focus on the destination. Letting go and embracing change is the best release.

No matter what you did, no matter who you are now or where you are, put out positive energy and continue doing things, whatever the result is. Know that complaining or hanging on to the past takes up energy; spend that energy on things that you enjoy instead. Sometimes you feel out of control of your life, but you have a responsibility to find something that you want to achieve in your life.

Remember your most meaningful experience without regrets and think of how you have grown into the strong person you are today.

'

Enjoy every moment in life; some things only happen once. Focus and count your blessings for today.

HANADI ALQATARI

Be happy and positive every day, even on the bad days. The art of enjoying life is not complicated. All we need to do is tune up our mind to enjoy moments of life and stay open to anything. Train yourself to see and think positively in every moment.

Stop running. Do your best to live in the present and think about how blessed you are that you can enjoy the things you already have.

'

'Keep going; your perfect life is waiting for you. Give yourself credit for all the energy you have to rediscover yourself.

HANADI ALQATARI

Being positive means being absolute, clear-cut, definite and forward-looking. Having positive thoughts towards something means creating thoughts that will transform energy into reality, even if you have previously tried and failed. Start small; start paying attention to your strength by wanting to change. It takes courage but will make you feel better. Put good energy into the world and remember there is something very special within you which will help you find your way to happiness.

It is never too late to create your happiness. Happy living means avoiding all the unpleasant things within us which make us unhappy.

You just need to know how to look inwards rather than looking outwards.

'When life does not seem to be going your way, decide to be an optimist and trust in your own actions.

HANADI ALQATARI

No matter how hard it may seem, encourage yourself to do the things you want to do for the future or today. Maybe you have difficulties with relationships or emotions and you are worrying about something. Try to remember that you have the capacity to control, to evolve, to be happy.

Of course sometimes we struggle to know how to deal with something. Trust in your own actions. Making the choice to shift your thinking about the struggles you are experiencing, even if you are facing something difficult, gives you the power of control over your life.

When faced with adversity, we need true courage and hope to create our reality.

'

Forgive yourself, no matter how long it takes, as many times as it takes to find peace.

HANADI ALQATARI

Forgiveness is a process that is different for everyone. Sometimes you need to hit rock bottom to open yourself up to the acceptance that can lead emotional healing.

Too many times you will feel sorry for things that you really do not need to feel guilt for. Accept what has passed; write down how you would have done things differently if you could go back and do it again. It will get better.

Believing in your own worth allows you to move on and truly forgive yourself.

'

When it seems easiest to give up and stay where you are, do not let this idea make you feel you are not good enough to do what you want to do.

HANADI ALQATARI

The key to happiness is having dreams. Allow yourself to think about every single thing you truly want. You only have one life; remember that it is never too late to start in this moment to pursue and live your dreams.

Change your perception of what 'dream' means to you. Dreams are not just fantasy; they can be achieved. It doesn't matter what your situation is.

The best feeling is doing something each day to work towards your dream.

'

Being a good example will lead to happiness.

HANADI ALQATARI

Setting a good example is not trying to change someone. Some people will follow your actions, while others won't. The more you practise the positive attitude you wish to see in others, the more you will encourage others to do the same.

Be nice to other people; tell someone they look beautiful; tell your friends and family how much you love them; stop gossiping; be kind to all around you. If you want to be a good example, believe in yourself. Remember that people appreciate positivity and it takes one small step to show it.

You do not have to be perfect. Regardless of your past mistakes, the best thing you can do is live by a good example and become an inspiration to others.

'

Every time you get upset at something, ask yourself: if you were to die tomorrow, was it worth wasting your time being angry?

UNKNOWN

Do you think that happy people are lucky or just born like that? Or you may think having money or an attractive personality makes you happier. Happiness is an attitude that you can adopt.

Give yourself the confidence to see your inner beauty and know that nobody else has what you have.

From now, make a difference and start to show your positive thoughts to the world.

'

Everything happens for a reason. Many things and people will cross your path. That is part of our spiritual lifestyle.

HANADI ALQATARI

Sometimes things happen to you that may seem painful and unfair at first, but when you think more about them you may come to understand that they helped you realise your potential, strength, willpower and heart. Learning to look for the reason behind things is part of the spirituality of human life. Sometimes you need a spiritual awakening; you must believe in your spirituality, your connection to every other living creature. All things are utterly connected.

Each important event in our life happens for a cause.

> *Everyone's journey is different. Explore what is right in front of you.*

HANADI ALQATARI

Who am I? Who do I want to be? It is wonderful to be a dreamer, but sometimes things go wrong.

Each of us has a path chosen for us, and it is up to you to walk the paths available to you and decide which ones will keep you going. Life is a journey, an experience. Stop comparing where you are now with where everyone else is. Stay open to your journey. You are not normal, and you do not need to be. Your own journey is right for you and will not be necessarily right for someone else.

Your life is not right or wrong, or good or bad. It is just different. Every life is unique. New experiences will add to the person you are; trust that you are on the right path when they occur. But make sure that you are taking steps towards where you want to be.

Your life is not meant to look like anyone else's. Be proud of it. Try different things to achieve your goals; deal with them in your own way.

'

When everything goes wrong, remember things will get better with time.

HANADI ALQATARI

Sometimes life closes doors to create a chance to grow even stronger. When you go through difficult times, remember that with every passing day you will see things differently.

Patience is not about waiting; it is the ability to keep a good attitude while working hard on your dreams, knowing that the hard times will surely pass and something wonderful is on its way to you.

'

Happiness is not the absence of problems, but the ability to deal with them.

HANADI ALQATARI

Every day, people struggle; they experience pain and anxiety. The challenge here is how to react. Take the action that will help you to move on; be thoughtful and bring your problems closer to resolution. Unhappy people do not make choices; they react negatively to everything, complain and choose nothing. Once you choose to speak, see and deal with things positively, you allow happiness into your life, and you equip yourself to respond to whatever life may throw at you.

By taking your problems as a road map to happiness, you will realise that you hold the key to your own happiness.

> *To find the happiness that you seek, stand in front of the mirror and tell yourself, 'I have everything I need inside me.'*

HANADI ALQATARI

Everything in your reality is only a mirror of your feelings. Happiness cannot be found; it can only be made, and you cannot change what the mirror reflects unless you make your own happiness. All the emotions that you have are a choice, but simply knowing that happiness is a choice is not enough. You must begin to practise creating inner peace in your everyday life.

You are the main source of your happiness. Remember that no one but you can take away your happiness and your inner peace.

Happiness is not found in anything outside ourselves. You should learn to be happy right here, right now, and that happiness should be found within.

> # Just because you fail once doesn't mean you're gonna fail at everything.

MARILYN MONROE

Whatever you are going through in life, you should keep in mind that failure is a necessary stepping stone to achieving your dreams. Every one of us is going to fail every once in a while, but it is never too late to stand up again and continue to do what we love.

There are failures that might knock us down to the ground. I have found, in times like this, that it's best to focus on dealing with whatever immediate obstacles are in my path.

Not having the money, weight or status that you expected or that society expects is not failure. Failure is when you give up.

If you fail, think about what lessons that failure has taught you and how you can do better next time.

'

'When things do not work out, something better is coming.

HANADI ALQATARI

It is good to have plans, ideas and dreams, but they will not always turn out as you imagine. The problem is not that life is unfair; it is our broken idea of fairness. Of course you need to remind yourself that you are indeed deserving of genuinely good things and happiness in your life, but you will look back and realise that every little thing that didn't work out added up and brought you somewhere wonderful.

Sometimes things not working out the way you wanted them to is a wonderful stroke of luck.

'

Everyone feels sad from time to time. No matter how hopeless you feel, do not listen to the things you tell yourself when you are sad.

HANADI ALQATARI

Sad feelings come and go; some last only a moment and some last longer. Lots of different things could cause sadness, for example when something does not work out the way you hoped, but sadness doesn't mean that all hope is lost. It means you are being tested and taught. When you have that kind of hope in you, your struggles will lead you to strength and your dreams will be fulfilled.

Do not wait for sadness to pass. If you have a negative mindset, every day will be a struggle. If you feel that you cannot do anything about sadness, remind yourself that you have the inner guidance to keep going, and continue with the hope of gaining control over it.

'

When you are positive and challenge yourself to see the good in every situation, you begin to bring joy and happiness to your life.

HANADI ALQATARI

It is not always easy, but it's important to remember that there is a purpose for every situation. How you control your attitude and choose to feel about it is up to you. It is up to you to find the good, to be positive and to stand up for the things you believe in regardless of what is happing around you.

Nothing positive could come from blaming your situation for all your problems or even blaming yourself. Stop playing the blame game and start dealing with life, even when the situation is bad and things are difficult. Train yourself to see the good in life. Practise being positive.

No matter what situation you may find yourself in, you always can see something good if you take the time to think about it.

'

Every single action you take
can have a big impact on
the world.

HANADI ALQATARI

Our thoughts, feelings, beliefs, ideas, even our relationships with each other can really make a difference and change our world for the better.

Each one of us plays our own part in creating a brighter world. Ask yourself, 'What can I do today to make this world better?' It is simple for every one of us to take action to improve our life and the lives of others.

You just need to apply yourself, so start now. There is always hope. Feel inspired to start doing your part in making a difference.

Happiness is a choice.
Choose to be happy.

HANADI ALQATARI

Being happy does not mean that everything's going perfectly; it means that when your faith and strength are challenged you are able to appreciate what is in front of you. Each one of us has the most incredible ability to take control of our happiness.

Happiness can be simple when you decide to learn how to be happy.

Every time something goes wrong, look around you and start to measure the good things in your life. You will find that everything you could ever want is actually in front of you.

Today, choose to be happy and you will notice that all the people around you will do the same.

'*When times get tough, people will show you who they really are. Some people will leave you and some will help you to improve your life when you need it.*

HANADI ALQATARI

Some relationships are difficult, some relationships are blessings, some will teach you something, some will test you and some will bring out the best in you.

Never regret knowing anyone. Instead, appreciate those who care for you, who love you and who always stand beside you.

There are lots of people around you when times are easy. But when you are down in life, you get to know who is standing by your side and who your true friends are.

'

If you do not go for what you want, you will never achieve your goals.

HANADI ALQATARI

L earn how to take control of your own goals. If you are writing down ideas of how you can make your dreams happen, you are already a success because thinking and planning will motivate you to reach your goals.

If, for example, you're drawing up a plan to lose weight, you may need to break that single large goal into several smaller steps that are more easily achievable on their own. Setting smaller, less intimidating goals will help you to reach the overall goal that you've set.

Always create a picture of what you want in your life, start working on it and stay motivated as you achieve each step.

'

You do not have to plan everything in your life. Sometimes you need to let the situation be what it is and trust that there will be better days in your life.

HANADI ALQATARI

If you find yourself being turned down for something good, something unexpected happens that changes your plans or you otherwise find yourself having a hard time, you might feel like everything is going wrong and start to think like you will be stuck in this bad situation forever. You cannot control everything. Sometimes you just need to relax, release control and believe that you are not rejected; you are redirected to something better and bigger.

Whatever unexpected challenges may come your way, have faith that things will work out and trust what the universe has in store for you.

Why spend time worrying, fighting, regretting?

All you have to do is believe.

'

Even if things are not perfect, be happy.

HANADI ALQATARI

Our lives do not always turn out exactly the way we want. Sometimes we feel like life is against us.

If you want to live a happy life, remember that happiness comes from inside. That your feelings reflect your thoughts.

Whenever something seems to go wrong, practise giving yourself a break to look inside.

Remember, you are strong enough to live each day to the fullest. It is not up to life to make you happy. Happiness already within you; you make yourself happy.

> *You will never get what you want if you do not give yourself permission to feel free.*

Success comes in understanding that the things you do each day are your choice alone. So often in life we do things we do not want to do or make certain choices because we keep telling ourselves that we have 'no choice'. We are afraid to chase our dreams because we fear others will judge us or reject us.

If you allow others or circumstances to control your choices, it will be hard to have a true choice in anything you do.

Be free to pursue your goals; be free to give your time and energy to things you deserve.

If one day you struggle with being free in your decisions and actions, you can start all over again by giving yourself that freedom to choose what you want.

'

Focus and think about the abundance in your life. Do not limit your life choices. There are infinite ways to live happily.

HANADI ALQATARI

We do not give ourselves enough time to think how good life really is for us. Some have more than others, but in the end you have to remember to focus more on the good things in your life. If anything seems to be lacking, it's the lack of appreciation.

Look at the abundance that is there for you. Perhaps you have healthy food, a good family, trustworthy friends, a safe home to live in, enough money.

Abundance is all around us, if we just take the time to recognise it.

'

Old ways will not open new doors; you just have to get out of your own way.

UNKNOWN

I would not be where I am today if I did not step outside my comfort zone and embrace change. Our life experiences are what shape us. Trying something new can inspire us and open us to new chances that we never imagined.

When you feel stuck or bored, try new ways. If you never start to take the chances you need for your happiness and wellbeing, you will never get somewhere.

‘

Busy yourself with what you want to achieve, not with negativity or drama.

HANADI ALQATARI

If you want to feel happy and inspired each day, you will need to busy yourself by working with a positive strength of purpose towards your own dreams, avoiding any negativity and sensational drama.

Being busy doesn't always mean real work; it can be any simple activity that will inspire you with a feeling of excitement to help you succeed in your personal goals.

Be busy loving your life, put your heart and energy into it, but do not rush through it.

Free yourself from feeling fragile and broken.

HANADI ALQATARI

How many times a day do you force yourself not to worry, not to feel depressed or angry? These feelings are usually the result of sitting and dwelling on what has happened to you, or on current anxieties: struggles with your living conditions, trouble at work or conflict with someone, for example.

Replaying negative scenarios and negative thoughts in your head, whether these thoughts are connected to the past or the present, will allow the stress to become a habit.

Any time you are feeling overwhelmed, broken or stressed, try to ask yourself: is there a real problem? If there is, can you take steps to solve that problem? Even if there's no clear solution, there are steps you can take to make yourself feel better. Express what you feel, share what happened and start to feel emotionally free because you are no longer holding on.

If it happened in the past then it is dead and gone.

You can shift negative thoughts to positive through exercise. Walk, hike, bike, work out at the gym. These activities will make you feel good, which in turn will lead to good thoughts.

Love

'

Love is always worth fighting for. Start loving more.

HANADI ALQATARI

There is so much power in love. Love will bring you energy when it takes hold of you.

Love is about true feeling towards our family and friends. Each and every one of us has our own true love deep down inside for the people who are important in our lives.

When you give yourself the permission to love more, your life will bring you an abundance of blessings that can be compared to nothing else.

'*Following our heart means living in tune with our heart and being in love with our decisions.*

HANADI ALQATARI

There will be times in your life when your intuition tells you one thing, while your mind disagrees. All the intuition that comes from your heart will tell you to do something. Something that defies logic, totally different from other people's thinking.

You do it. Listen to your intuition. Do not let the complications and the noise of others' opinions drown out your inner voice. Ignore logic; the decision is up to you. Give power to your heart by making decisions with a wide open heart.

Sometimes we need the courage to let this deep impulse drive us.

This is not 'thinking with your heart'. Keep your mind for creative works and complicated problems, and allow your heart to take care of your happiness and your personal/spiritual development.

Starting to think this way will encourage your heart to speak out.

We are not apart from each other; we are all connected with love in different ways that make us all the same.

HANADI ALQATARI

We have to stop letting our differences divide us. Each of us has different thoughts, different abilities, different ways of reacting to situations, but the same spirit. We are all unique in our own way. The ability to love each other will let us live in the greatest peace of heart and soul.

We have to decide to accept our differences in loving ways. Our differences are complementary.

'

Those you love will go through hard times. Don't give up on them. Patience + caring + empathy = love.

BRENDON BURCHARD

Love is loving someone for who they are, who they were and who they will be. I am so blessed with what my beloved ones have done, are doing and will do to keep me strong. Even when my situation is frustrating, they understand me and know what I need without asking.

When you are by someone who loves you as you are and may be different from you in many ways, continuing to love them will be one of the best decisions you ever make.

They say love is blind.
I disagree. Infatuation is
blind. Love is all-seeing
and accepting.

There have been times in my life when I was feeling lost, confused and worrying about everything. Today I have begun to understand how love can make a difference.

Love is positive emotion, which you share with another person: any person you want.

Shout out to your loved ones and let everyone you love know that you love them.

There is no feeling so great as love.

'We can have the intent to love others, but without initiative, without real acts of respect, caring, and affection for another, intention alone remains useless. Soulless. Thinking is not love; giving is.*

BRENDON BURCHARD

I have learnt that expressing love on your own initiative is the most powerful and precious thing you have to give. It is an easy thing to love others, but a true lover knows that *showing* love is important to any relationship.

There are millions of different ways to express your feelings.

Remember actions speak louder than words. Think about someone you love and tell them your feelings. Reach them and watch how that changes you for the better.

'

Fall in love with someone who wants you, who waits for you. Who understands you even in the madness; someone who helps you and guides you; someone who is your support, your hope. Fall in love with someone who talks with you after a fight. Fall in love with someone who misses you and wants to be with you. Do not fall in love only with the idea of being in love.

UNKNOWN

One of the hardest things to deal with in a relationship is staying with someone just because you are afraid to be alone.

It is not enough just to hear, 'I love you.' If someone loves you, they have to put in time and effort and demonstrate their love through both their words and their actions.

Pay attention to how your partner acts and speaks to know how much they care about you. As great as being in love can feel, remember you are a unique woman with a beating heart, and not everyone deserves that heart.

'*I love people who make me laugh. I honestly think it is the thing I like most, to laugh. It cures a multitude of ills. It is probably the most important thing in a person.*

AUDREY HEPBURN

Most of us live lives filled with responsibilities, but life is too short to spend stressing ourselves out.

People who make you laugh are often the ones who help you when you are in need, and they genuinely care.

Enjoy where you are now and here, and do your best to surround yourself with people who will make you laugh even when times are hard.

'

Love changes the whole
climate of your inner being,
and with that change the
whole existence is changed.

OSHO

If you want to make a difference in your life, start to love yourself and it will make you love the world around you. Even small tasks in life need all our love.

No matter what happens to you, keep giving yourself credit for everything you do and see what it brings back for you.

Sometimes it is difficult to give up on being perfect and begin the journey of loving your true self. This part of the journey will simply return you to the peaceful feeling of being you.

Remind yourself that no one will remember your imperfections; they will remember your kindness and the love you are giving them.

'

Love knows how to go into the unknown. Love knows how to throw all securities. Love knows how to move into the unfamiliar and the uncharted.

Love is courage. Trust love.

OSHO

Everything we do in our life requires all forms of love. Happy or even painful as it may seem, love is something we all value the experience of.

Every being and everything is set in motion by love, and it keeps us growing emotionally and spiritually, fully awake and alive.

When you believe that all you need is love, you will feel deeply connected to everything around you and your heart and soul will soar.

'No matter how old you get, never stop dancing, never stop having fun, and never stop being in love.

HANADI ALQATARI

Never stop giving yourself a chance to fly. Respect yourself enough to be cheerful and happy in whatever situation you may find yourself in.

You deserve all the happiness and love in the world. Don't regret lost moments when you were younger; create new moments here, now. Keep on working your hardest to achieve your own happiness with all the madness and passion in your soul.

Listen to a happy, upbeat song and dance. Never stop smiling, because you never know who will fall in love with your smile.

'

Love is the only thing that activates our intelligence and our creativity, that purifies and liberates us.

PAULO COELHO

Love allows us to confront things and make all things possible. It empowers us; it calls on a spirit power.

We are here on this earth to experience love wherever we go.

Expand your heart with love and love fearlessly with all your heart.

Love is the only hope of the world.

OSHO

Look back on memories of hard times when you felt hopeless, and remember how love gave you strength and hope.

Whatever you are fighting today, you should always listen to your heart and ask yourself what it is that you really want. Sometimes love is all the guidance you need. Go where your heart takes you.

When you hope for something, let the door open for love. You will find love is a powerful emotion when you really experience it.

Stay away from people who carry a negative spirit. Spend your time with the people you love.

HANADI ALQATARI

Surround yourself with people who encourage you, support your ideas and bring out the best in you.

We've all faced negative people who bring us down and drain our energy, but, whatever you do, do not complain. Focus on solutions. It might be worth letting them know about the impact their behaviour has on you. If they are not willing to analyse and adjust their attitude, the best approach is not to spend so much time with them. Let the negativity pass.

All you need is to stay with the ones who support you and make you feel stronger with their love.

'

Count the things that you love and let the world know how much love you have inside you.

HANADI ALQATARI

Name the things you love in your life; perhaps write a list. Stay focused on the people or things you love in your life.

There are little things in life that are worth a lot more in the deep love they inspire than, for example, material objects.

Take a look at the lovely moments you've been having, people you love or simple things that you love the most. It is important to show love for all these things or people in your life. It helps you feel good.

Be brave, open your heart and show love openly. It will bring more blessings to your life.

Do it and feel it now.

'

*The strong woman is wise
enough to realise that her
struggles and challenges make
her stronger, but still has a
loving soul.*

HANADI ALQATARI

You become stronger with age and experience. Be grateful for your strength, and keep growing and learning to reach your goals. But without love your strength will not sustain you.

Love is a very powerful thing; it can remind you that you can be the strongest person in the world. Believing in the power of your own ability to love will make you stronger than you have ever been.

Keep loving more and more, even if you've been hurt by love. Remember that love is a powerful force and an amazing experience.

'

Your emotional intelligence is created when you begin to love with all your heart. Let love win.

HANADI ALQATARI

Love empowers us and gave us special strength during hard times. It brings us together. Everything becomes possible when carried out with love.

Express your love with your family, friends or co-workers. Do it now, not only on special occasions. Use love to give your actions greater meaning. You will be grateful that you are spreading love and becoming open to receiving love.

> *Appreciation is a kind of love that makes us see the beauty in what is in front of us.*

HANADI ALQATARI

Be that person who always knows how to connect with others in your life and tell them, 'Thank you for being part of my life.'

Appreciate every blessing in your life. Value every new blessing that comes your way.

Being appreciative of every day and expressing appreciation to every person around you is part of being happy.

It is time to connect with your family, friends and colleagues to tell them how you appreciate them, and in doing so you will teach them how to express their own appreciation too.

'

Time is precious. Spend it wisely with the people you love.

HANADI ALQATARI

You are happiest when you increase the time you spend with people you love. Never waste a minute thinking about people you do not like. There are always windows of opportunity open to reach out to any person you love.

There is no right or wrong way to spend your time, but you have the choice to spend time with the people who bring you comfort.

Whatever you are busy with, take action and find the time to do what you love with the people you love.

Make happy memories now.

'

Don't set yourself on fire to keep others warm.

UNKNOWN

We've all heard this; we need to love ourselves and have 'me time' before we can love and give to others.

Loving yourself isn't about the way you look; it is about the way you feel. You may have had emotional pain in your life, but you should feel the love and visualise the best self that lies within you.

'

Just knowing who you are,
deciding what you want and
loving yourself, you will
live an empowered life.

HANADI ALQATARI

When life knocks you down, look inside yourself and find the strength to face your situation.

Love yourself. You have been blessed with uniqueness and talent. Face your fears; it is not scary to figure out who you are and to take steps towards your dreams.

It is important to empower yourself by knowing how to distinguish who you are and what you want. Then your dreams will work for you.

‘

If you allow yourself to discover the power of love, you will find the master key to success.

HANADI ALQATARI

Love is an immensely powerful feeling that allows you to experience bliss, joy and a true relationship with the world around you.

Whatever your goals, whether you want to look and feel healthier, be thinner, strengthen your friendships or be more financially secure, the way to live the best life you can is to choose love. That is the key to getting anything you want.

> *When you let your ego go,
> you will allow the doors of
> love to open.*
>
> HANADI ALQATARI

Love is not romance; it is a powerful energy. Your heart is the centre of love. When you open your heart to see, taste, touch and feel you will start to experience love with people, animals, trees and rocks.

Each one of us has our own thoughts and feelings. If you create your life by choosing to strengthen your heart, you need to be loving, caring, compassionate, grateful and giving.

When your ego tells you that love is dangerous, stay open-hearted by holding love blameless and believing that love creates only goodness and beauty.

Soft-hearted people are really strong on the inside, no matter how the world sees them. Continue to practise kindness.

HANADI ALQATARI

There are times in life when you will experience grief and anger, or maybe you will cry a lot over people who have broken your heart. These are common experiences. But never be apologetic for who you are.

Do not hide your emotions; there is strength in weakness. And the real power is in not letting the world take away your softness.

Be proud that you have a soft heart in a cruel world. There is nothing better than softness and kindness.

'

Learn to do what you love.
If you have not found it, keep
searching for what elevates
your life energy.

HANADI ALQATARI

When you do what you love and love what you do, it will make you happy and light up your days. Start rearranging your days and weeks to allow more time for doing the things you not only enjoy but find purpose in.

It is easy to spend your spare time doing things you love. Write, read, learn a foreign language, play, cook, learn a new type of dance, meet old friends, arrange a party, plan for a trip, do anything that excites and energises you.

Do not make excuses; use your spare time. There is no end of activities and experiences to bring into your life. Find the ones you love.

'

True happiness comes from giving to the people whom you love, not from what you can get from them.

HANADI ALQATARI

One of the biggest joys in life is learning to inspire and encourage the people you surround yourself with. You cannot change people, but you can guide them onto a path that benefits them.

You might find that you want to be supportive but do not know how to. You may need to make positive changes to bring out the best in others.

I guarantee, once you have chosen to support the people around you, you will be better off.

Support is power.

'

*Your mind and imagination
are a creative force in your life.
Make sure the thoughts you
think are positive. They affect
what happens to you.*

HANADI ALQATARI

Through the power of your directed thoughts, you can create anything you want. Learn to control the nature of your habitual thoughts. Believe in your own ability to achieve the things you want.

I spoke earlier of the power of thoughts, but using thought really is an immensely powerful method that I personally use whenever I need it. It always works with amazing immediacy. When you control your thoughts and believe that anything is possible, you will achieve whatever you work towards.

Even when you use the power of your thoughts, do not forget to use your emotions and feel love inside. Know that the thoughts' power comes from within.

‘

Treat everyone with dignity,
with the same level of love
and respect regardless of their
social position or power.

HANADI ALQATARI

When you are down, you probably want others to be compassionate and kind toward you. You should offer that same compassion to others.

Put people on an equal footing and treat them with respect. You are no better or worse than anyone else. Each person has as much worth as you do; you should not do anything to anyone that you yourself would not want done to you.

It is also worth remembering that other people are not obliged to share your beliefs. In the end each person has to be their own person. You should give them respect without prejudice.

'

There are two ways to create your life: either through fear or through love. The choice is yours.

HANADI ALQATARI

We must learn how to build our life from inside out. No matter what happens, do not forget to recognise your own depth and power, and follow your bliss. Each action you take will usually be better than the previous one if you pay attention to the emotions and sensibilities that are flowing through your heart.

Sometimes, when you are stuck in a difficult situation, fear gives you an excuse to hide behind your heart. How many times have we failed in something because of our fear? Do not listen to your fears. Release your expectations of what should happen for you; trust in your instincts and your inner power to choose.

Moving forward brings you power to face your fear with love. Keep in mind Osho's great advice: *Move the way love makes you move.*

'*Notice who is around you and who is not. Appreciate those who make your soul blossom and be grateful to those who do not appreciate and respect your presence; they give you room in the space they abandoned.*

HANADI ALQATARI

As human beings, no one is born free from the need for love and support from others. We do not need anyone else to complete us, but we need to realise just how important it is to try our hardest to reach out and help each other. Each of us has our standards for what makes us feel loved.

While we need to learn to depend on ourselves for happiness, there is nothing wrong with feeling appreciated and seeing the love all around us. Value the people who are there for you and accept compassion from those who are willing to give it.

We all deserve to feel loved by the people in our lives.

Think about any dream or goal you really want. Turn it into a burning desire in your heart. Use the power of love to make it happen.

HANADI ALQATARI

When you focus on a goal and build a burning desire towards that goal, you will be able to keep moving towards it.

We need a little motivation to look at what we really want in life. Look at the goals that burn inside you in order to give yourself direction towards what you really want. Once you know what you want, once you truly desire it, then you can achieve it.

What is your biggest dream? Turn it into a burning desire in your heart.

'

Your heart wants to move but your body doesn't want to, so you are not lazy. Start dreaming again, get motivated by love and everything will be well.

HANADI ALQATARI

We sometimes get laziness and a lack of motivation mixed up. There's nothing wrong with taking quiet times where you sit and give yourself the peace you need and deserve, but sometimes the thing you really want to do feels like a burden.

I personally like to think of dreaming, inspiration and the love that comes from within as a type of motivation. There are many types of motivation, but I find motivation by love is very helpful in pushing me to do things.

'*We love life whenever
we can.*

MAHMOUD DARWISH

Enjoy every moment you live now. Do not be held back by what happened before.

Sometimes changing your life feels impossible and you repeat the same mistakes over and over again. First of all, know what you really want and need. Believe in yourself and get ready to start to live the life you love, no matter what!

'

Kindness is a practice, not a project, that leads you to a happy life.

HANADI ALQATARI

Kindness is a form of inspiration that comes from the heart. When you have it in your mind to extend kindness to others, you will feel fully empowered to create positive changes in your daily life.

Challenge yourself to practise kindness. You will feel all your acts of kindness bring an exciting sense of inner peace. It is so wonderful to reach into the heart and soul of another person.

Life is not fair; it never will be. Little acts of kindness will make us believe in our own empowerment and strength. We are able to help others and be the giving heart.

'

Love your family; they are the only friends who will listen without judgment.

HANADI ALQATARI

Being around family brings pleasure to both you and them. No matter how many people you have in your life, you can balance each and every relationship. It is not necessary to be like your family members or to feel they need to be like you; their personalities are their personalities. Let them be, and love them for everything they are and are not. Accepting them with all of their flaws can help maintain a strong, healthy relationship with the best supports in your life.

Lack of communication increases distance. Taking time to communicate with family can improve your mood and strength, and it will have the same effect on your beloved family.

'*When we do certain things for our beloved people, we do not expect rewards.*

HANADI ALQATARI

When I did something as simple as just being there for a friend who was struggling, I could not believe how such a small thing brought both of us so much happiness.

Giving is helping others just because you care, without expectation in return. The joy of being able to make a positive impact on someone's life becomes its own reward.

Do one thing for someone you love and give from your generous heart. It will come back around to you in some kind of peace and love. Our hearts are free to show love to our beloved people and let them know they are not alone.

'

Some people teach you how to love. Be open to receive that love and those warm feelings toward you.

HANADI ALQATARI

There are times in our lives when we say harsh things to people who love us and we find ourselves putting caveats on love, just because things are not going our way.

What would the world be like if we understood more deeply that love is necessary to experience power, happiness and inner peace? If you find someone loves you unconditionally, loves you just for who you are, makes you feel peace with yourself and gives you strength, let your heart open wide to receive that love.

Love is receiving and giving emotion. Allow others to express their feelings toward you.

And remember, if you struggle to receive love, it can become hard to then give it out.

'

You are worthy and lovable.
Love and accept yourself
with all the mistakes you
have made.

HANADI ALQATARI

We all want to be loved and accepted, but that has to start with us. Your own self-respect is all you need to deal with whatever is thrown at you. We cannot find love unless we believe we are lovable. I believe that every time we feel good about what we do, we will actually become more respected.

Tell yourself today that you can be happy here, inside yourself, just as you are, by freeing yourself of any negative emotion.

'

*There is only one way to
achieve great love: choose to
love openly and fearlessly.*

HANADI ALQATARI

Think about why we do what we do for love.

To gain a deeper understanding of how to love another and to be loved, we must know that our capacity to fearlessly love another starts with courage in our heart. Do not expect others to read your feelings. Fearlessly express your feelings and emotions.

It is an incredible thing to keep offering love to everyone fearlessly, but it is possible, because love is infinite.

Know that showing your love through words and actions with no expectations is loving fearlessly.

‘ Give love freely.

HANADI ALQATARI

This will allow you to see the abundance in your world that you may be missing right now. If you care about the happiness of people around you without expectation, you will be grateful that you are able to make them feel valued and worthy. This free giving is the energy that creates more of what we love in our lives.

Love is happiness and appreciation. It allows us to become more open; it empowers us to heal all wounds and appreciate all of the abundance currently in our lives. It creates gratitude for every relationship, enabling it to succeed.

Each one of us is unique in our way of loving, but all of us are capable of giving without expectations.

'

Do not miss your chance to tell the people who matter how much they mean to you.

HANADI ALQATARI

Time goes by so fast. Do not wait until you are out of time. Leaving things left unsaid can destroy relationships. Feelings and emotions are energies moving through your body; if not expressed and released, they can cause a negative impact on your health. Share feelings you've hidden and express your emotions at any time with the people you love and feel grateful for.

Do not be afraid of what you might say. Whatever the result is, you will get back what you put into any relationship and will find peace in knowing you've done right.

'

*Love yourself for who you are,
even if you are different.*

HANADI ALQATARI

Sometimes others will make comments about you. No matter what you do or say, there will always be someone bound to make a comment. The most important thing is to know that the comments people make are a reflection of themselves.

We all have days when we feel down and think there is something wrong with us. It is very hard to be yourself when your society pressures you to be like other people, but remember to be kind to yourself if you decide to change.

Do not forget there is a reason why you were made the way you are. This will give you the chance to grow stronger and happier by accepting and loving yourself.

*Most things we work toward
in our life are based on the
idea of wanting love and
acceptance.*

UNKNOWN

Respect your emotions and feelings by showing someone that you need them. Even if you are strong and emotionally independent, needing someone is essential for your wellbeing.

Let love in by being open to receiving support from loved ones. Be brave by opening up to someone you love.

Tell someone how you really feel and how much you appreciate their presence in life.

'

Life is short, so never stop doing little things for yourself. Notice what you love, not what you hate. Happiness is enjoying small things every day fully.

HANADI ALQATARI

No matter how good or bad you have it, instead of spending your time worried about what you are missing in your life, try to focus on what you would love to do in your life today. Live every moment in your life with love in your heart; enjoy the little things. One day you will look back and appreciate these moments when you reflect on days gone by.

Small pleasures in life can be the happiest moments, but often you don't notice them unless you realise that moment is over.

Bringing more love into your life will make both your inner beauty and your outer beauty shine.

HANADI ALQATARI

You are ready to understand love's true meaning when your heart is ready to practise giving more love. You will attract love into your life when you are willing to give. So practise getting love by giving it. Love is who you are inside. If your heart is filled with love, love will be a reflection of who you are.

'

You wake up every day to fight the same emotional pain, depression, anxiety and anger. Love is what ultimately heals you.

HANADI ALQATARI

Sometimes we find ourselves going through difficult times, feeling anxiety or stress that drains our energy, hope and drive. If you spend your time waiting for the magical solution or trying to pretend your feelings do not exist, you could end up feeling worse.

Many of us, if not most, carry emotional scars.

While much emotional pain requires time or thoughtful solutions to heal, some pain can be healed by truly feeling love within.

Love is the solution if we are willing to open up. It gives the energy to live a life worth living.

Negative people need love.

UNKNOWN

The action of others can sometimes hurt you, for example when people close to you mistreat you or avoid you. Letting someone know that they have hurt you by their actions can be difficult.

If you have someone negative in your life, the best thing to do for yourself may be to walk away. However, some of these people are tough on the outside but may be soft and warm on the inside. If you believe in their potential to be better, it is your challenge to rise above their negative attitude and try to show love and give positive attention to them. Take the time to understand them; that is often exactly what they need. Offer love even if you feel it will be rejected; remember negative people often have difficulty receiving love from others because they feel unlovable, so do not take their rejection of your love personally.

Be able to love others. It is the best way to release the negative feelings inside them.

Practise loving kindness.

HANADI ALQATARI

Practising loving kindness can help you to develop feelings of goodwill and love towards yourself and others. When we look at ourselves we will find that many of us do not take as good care of ourselves as we should. The more we take care of our emotional, physical and spiritual health, the stronger the sense of love and kindness we can feel for ourselves, and that will lead us to give love to the people in our lives.

Love is within us, around us and between us. As loving kindness is a heart meditation practice, which helps us to develop the quality of loving acceptance, begin with loving acceptance of yourself. Be ready to show love, respect and kindness toward others in all situations and relationships.

Even a small dose of loving kindness can uplift our hearts.

'

Whatever you focus on, you will attract in your life. As you feel ... you vibrate.

HANADI ALQATARI

Focusing on the things you want in your heart will bring those things into your life. You can use your heart energy to create your most profound desires. To make your wishes come true you will need to find positive ways of energising your heart. The stronger and more focused the positive feelings, the stronger the dream becomes.

Concentrate on each feeling to examine how it really feels inside you. This will show you just how powerful your heart feelings are, and how much they impact on your thoughts, both energising your heart to feel great.

Focusing on your feelings is a great way to reach out to your dreams. Listen to the feelings in your heart; they are central to making dreams come true.

Remember your heart holds your personal power to make your dream a reality. The energy in your heart will work like magic to attract what you need if you balance the thoughts in your mind and feelings in your heart.

'

Be so busy loving the life you've got that there is no time for regret and moaning about your problems.

HANADI ALQATARI

It is easy to let the past steal our present and future from us, but you are not your mistakes and you are not your struggles. You have the power to accept and feel love for your life.

Today and this moment are all we have. Practise loving the unique life that you have. You are not able to choose everything that happens to you, but you can find comfort in spending time doing the things you love to do.

Loving your own beautiful journey will give you happiness.

Judge nothing, you will
   be happy.
Forgive everything, you will
   be happier.
Love everything, you will
   be happiest.

SRI CHINMOY

Peace, understanding, supporting, encouraging and helping: it is all about love, which relates to different forms of profound kindness.

There will be times in your life when you are told to do something that upsets your plans and your emotions. When that happens, do it with love and ignore everything else.

Remember it is your job to get up every morning and decide to make everything around you beautiful with the power of your love.

'

Smile and give from the heart.

HANADI ALQATARI

Whatever gifts or simple reasons to feel good we have been blessed with, why would we ever want to hide our happiness? Use it to smile no matter what.

Did you know that your smile has superpowers that can reduce stress and improve your health and mood? Do not think smiling is only the result of feeling happy. When you smile, even if you are faking it, it makes you feel happier.

Your smile has the power to open you up to opportunities and can change your entire day and that of everyone around you as well.

Allow your beauty to glow by wearing a smile on your face. A smile is a beautiful, special gift to give and to receive.

> *Have patience with those you love when they go through hard times. They need your support. Do not give up on them.*

HANADI ALQATARI

Understanding, caring for and having patience with your loved ones is a kind of unconditional love.

If someone you love is having a hard time, take the time to support them. Try to understand and know what they want without asking.

Accept them for who they are when they are struggling. Remind them your feelings towards them will not change, no matter what challenge they are facing right now; remind them they are no less a person just because they are going through a hard time; remind them that their difficulties are not their fault; remind them that you love them and will support them.

Sometimes all that matters is being around them.

Maybe their hard time is the time to recalibrate your relationship with them and help it grow stronger.

'

Good friends will pull you up,
hold you while you are failing
and encourage you in anything
that you try.

HANADI ALQATARI

There are two kinds of friends: fake friends who give only a little, and true or good friends who are helpful and let their light shine over you. These true friends are the people we seek to support us when we feel that all hope is lost. Most of us have good friends all around who will remain positive about our dreams and goals when we ask for their help and inspiration.

It is normal to feel lost, angry or confused some days. In this situation you must not hesitate to ask your true friends for their support.

You must remember that true friends will never make you feel guilty for needing them. They will not put you down but will encourage you to be a happy person through challenges.

'

Helping others and supporting them in their dreams and goals is the best way to love them.

HANADI ALQATARI

We all have dreams and goals we must fight for, but those who love are fighting for people who care for and who need them. They take care of their loved ones and encourage them to continue in the direction of their goals and dreams.

If we have dreams and goals for the sake of our family, children or friends, we must not wait to shine love on them. This may be the support they need to achieve their dreams.

'

If you do not inspire love in your heart each day you will experience emotional pain in your life.

HANADI ALQATARI

Often, when our actions make us loved or liked, we enjoy the happiness that comes only from giving positive emotions to others. Love shows up in every word we speak and every action we do for others, brightening our day and our mood.

Choose love to live an inspired life.

'

*Love is finding a balance
between taking and giving, and
doing our best to see it in our
lives and direct it towards the
people we love the most.*

HANADI ALQATARI

L ove opens the floodgates of our emotions to direct them outward and inward. We all take actions in our lives, but without love there is no courage inspiring us to move forward.

Love is within us and beyond us and seeing everything through the eyes of love. If we allow it to flow into our hearts, it will naturally flow out to others.

'

Love without getting hurt.

HANADI ALQATARI

If you are a person who loves to love, make sure this feeling of love leads you to the highest level of thinking and doing. You do not need to struggle to love or to be loving. Instead, act lovingly towards yourself and keep doing things that nurture you.

When people complain that love hurts, it hurts because we do not reach each other's expectations. That is why we feel disappointment or pain.

Remember, being in love is not about trying your hardest to cater to someone's needs and forgetting who you are. It is about doing the best for each other on both sides, and it is necessary to have your own life and goals that extend outside your relationship.

Connect your heart to your life.

HANADI ALQATARI

When you connect your heart to your life, there will be no more outward obstacles to living happily. Your inner world and outer world are mirrors of each other.

Whatever your situation is, whatever drama is going on around you, in your work, your family or your relationships, do not let any of it affect your inner homeostasis. Keeping the vibe at the level of peace is hard to do sometimes, especially when your days are not going according to your plan. Do not try to fix everything you do not like around you; instead tame the inner beast inside your head, and your outer world of events and relationships will reflect the highest level of happiness and joy.

Remember you can transform any chaotic situation into inner peace when you have reached the deepest level of your heart.

'

Through self-love, you are allowing others and the whole world to love you.

HANADI ALQATARI

If you believe in a sense of self-love and accepting yourself with the good and the bad, your potential for happiness is infinitely expanded.

Self-love is making time to do whatever you love, being serious about following the path that your soul is on.

Self-love is not blaming anyone for your current issues; it is trusting yourself to find genuine ways to be co-creator of your destiny.

Now, remember: if you are not practising self-love and simply being in the arms of your soul, even the best partner on the earth will not be able to make you feel happy and loved.

'

In every step you take in your life journey, give freely and treat others with respect. This will remind others to be kind to one another.

HANADI ALQATARI

Empowering others is your connection to life's infinite supply of energy. Being an agent of positive change for those around you helps you experience empathy and love.

Every nod, every smile, every word and action can be a positive force. Random acts of kindness will help you to find simplicity in your life.

Because happiness is simple.

Strength

'

I am not perfect, but I learnt how to deal with my imperfection.

HANADI ALQATARI

You do not need to be perfect to inspire others. Stop being unhappy with yourself.

Your happiness does not depend on others; just love who you are.

Once you find it is okay to be different, your life will change for the better and you will feel proud.

Try your best, get back up and believe the fact that no one is perfect.

Only in lifting others up shall you rise.

BRENDON BURCHARD

Many people have found strength to rise up by lifting others up or helping others in many ways, such as through great respect, positive thoughts, or being encouraging and understanding.

As women we are living in a fast-paced society filled with negativity and jealousy. If you want to make a real difference, start now to be the encouraging woman to others and focus on lifting others up.

Find the way now.

'

Sensitive people should be treasured. They love deeply and think deeply about life. They are loyal, honest and true. The simple things sometimes mean the most to them. They do not need change or harden. Their purity makes them who they are.

UNKNOWN

Be yourself and be who you are. This is the way I am living my life.

You may feel that your sensitivity is a weakness or be ashamed that others notice it. If we decide that our sensitivity is shameful or unacceptable, we will build a large wall between ourselves and those around us.

Hiding our feelings and trying to be someone else is unhealthy. All our feelings and emotions are beautiful and worth expressing.

> The Japanese say you have
>   three faces.
> The first face, you show to
>   the world.
> The second face, you show to
>   your close friends, and
>   your family.
> The third face, you never show
>   anyone. It is the truest
>   reflection of who you are.

UNKNOWN

At one point in my life I was trying to show my family, my friends and the world the best side of my personality and the most suitable face for those around me, but I found it was not the true me.

A few years later I understand that when we try to satisfy all around us, it will put us in a painful position and make us feel as if something is missing in our life. We can create the lives we dream of when we decide to be who we truly are.

'

Do not hesitate to set out on your own path just because you are afraid of being judged by others. People will still judge what you do.

HANADI ALQATARI

You have the ability to do what you love. Do not let anyone stop you pursuing what you believe in. Break out and distance yourself from anyone who says 'you can't' or 'you shouldn't'.

Stop looking for approval from others. If they continually judge or disapprove of what you do, you must be strong enough to stand up for what you need to be.

When you experience this amazing feeling, you will learn that it is a waste of time to listen to people who do not understand what you can do.

Replace your fear of judgment with a powerful feeling.

'

Appreciate your true friend if you have one, especially if she has stuck by your side through tough times. If you lose her, you may never find a replacement.

HANADI ALQATARI

Make a point of thanking your true friends if you have chosen good ones. Remember to be grateful for them and express your love and appreciation to every single friend who has been strong for you.

'

All happiness depends on courage and work.

HONORÉ DE BALZAC

What matters most is to keep working on yourself. There will be times you feel afraid that you are unable to do anything you want.

Refuse to give up, and stand up for what you believe inside your heart.

Each of us is born with the courage to take a small step each day towards our dreams.

'

Do not allow silly drama to stress you out. Breathe and let it go.

A lot of drama takes place in our heads. This is because we get caught up in our own worlds and let drama consume us. Drama is anything that causes you to lose your mental energy and peace.

I recently realised that I cannot control other people's drama and behaviour. The only person I can control is *me*, and I can let go of anyone who negatively influences my thoughts and actions.

Be a friend to yourself. When others' bad habits start affecting you, let the drama go by walking away.

'*Never let your dreams die simply because someone takes aim at you as you march to the mountaintop, do not falter and do not fear, for your courage will inspire us one day and all the cynics' dark comments will quickly fade in the bright sunlight of your contribution.*

BRENDON BURCHARD

It is okay to want your own happiness. It is okay to care about yourself the most. You are not obliged to sit there and smile and swallow every word that everyone heaps on you. You have everything you need to be what you want to be. Incredible change happens when you have the courage to control your own ideas. This means refusing to let anyone think or decide on your behalf.

You will face people in life who will say things to bring you down to their level. In these cases you will want to make them feel as bad as they have made you feel. But this is not the right reaction. Be patient and stop spending time with them. Keep your biggest goals close to your heart and give new meaning to every step you take.

With your capabilities and willingness to change, you will find that you are living a happy life you have built. And you will be amazed by how much you can inspire others.

'

You are accepted forever, just as you are.

OSHO

Accepting yourself and loving who you are is the source of many wonderful things. I am still learning every day how good it feels to love myself. There is so much life-changing power in realising that loving ourselves is not narcissistic, but rather enables us to re-evaluate the time that we are taking to do loving things for ourselves.

Love who you were, who you are and who you will be. Do one loving thing for yourself today and learn that loving yourself is not hard. Remember, there are people out there who think you are awesome.

> *Bring more art into the world.*
> *Your creative energy and*
> *contributions matter more*
> *than shuffling lame tasks. You*
> *are not a cog, you are a creator.*

BRENDON BURCHARD

You do not need to be talented to be an artist; you just need to take time to add value to what you do.

Each one of us is a unique, creative artistic person who can really bring our worth and positive impact into the world.

Art is an energy you could use to work towards your life's purpose.

Look around you at everything designed through the artistic process.

'

Being strong does not mean you do not feel pain. It means you feel it and try to understand it, so you can grow from it.

UNKNOWN

Pain is part of growing; it means you are growing stronger and wiser. It takes courage to move forward and accept change. Some types of pain can make us a different person, but in a good way, making positive changes and feeling more personal strength.

When I thought I was done growing, I thought my problems were over and done too. Then I realised that life is a journey, a process that is constantly presenting us with new difficulties to help us grow stronger, happier and more compassionate.

'

*When you truly do not care
what anyone thinks of you, you
have reached a dangerously
awesome level of freedom.*

UNKNOWN

Sometimes thoughts and fears of what others think of you will get too loud and it will be hard to hear yourself.

How others see you is not important. Do not waste your time trying to be what others want you to be. What people around you think of you cannot change who you are or what you are worth unless you allow it to.

Being different is what makes you special, and you are best at being yourself.

It is your life to live. The more relaxed you become with what you are, the more comfortable you will start to feel just being *you*.

'

Art is to console those who are broken by life.

VINCENT VAN GOGH

A rt is a part of our humanity. Art is what makes us human and provides us with ways to express ourselves.

Throughout history, our greatest inventors and scientists have merged their inventions and works with artistic creativity.

Art is everywhere, from the house we live in to the people we choose and the books we read. Open your soul and look around you and see the artistic beauty everywhere. Enjoy the colours you see around you, whether they are inside your house or out.

> *We all have those times when we break down. It is okay to cry because it cleanses the soul and gives you the courage to start anew.*

UNKNOWN

The beautiful thing about life is that there is always a new day to start again.

Do not worry about being worried, especially when you feel something is upsetting or something big goes down in your life. You must first accept your feelings; those feelings are a part of you. Understand any tears are just part of being human. You have everything you need inside you to live; just embrace all your emotions. There are people, there are shoulders to cry on.

Our feelings help us know we are alive. Let that make you happy.

> *Complaining and talking about our problems is a bad habit. What if we said something positive and talked about the joy in our life at the moment?*

HANADI ALQATARI

If you want to get over your problems, stop talking about them. Your mouth affects your mind and it will be difficult to find solutions. The more you talk about them, the more you think about them, which only causes you to miss out on all the joy and wonder in the present.

Make an effort to put good energy into the world. It will bring more joy than allowing the problem to grow.

The more joy you give, the more joy you attract. If you make the choice to talk only of your joys, you will create momentum for the others around you to do the same.

Complaining about problems is a hard addiction to break indeed.

'

Change is hard at first, messy in the middles and gorgeous at the end.

ROBIN SHARMA

Give yourself permission to start making changes to your life or yourself. If you do not like something in your life, you have to find the strength to change the way you think about it.

Change means you are growing up. Growing up means you are becoming a better person. Moving on does not take a day. Whether it be ten days or ten years from now, it is important to be mindful and have the courage to change your choices and actions.

Every day brings a chance to start a new chapter in our life, if we make the decision to change and improve ourselves.

If you have never experienced change, then begin the process of change now. You do not get the result unless you try.

> *The struggles and challenges
> are part of life. Accept
> whatever comes your way.
> It is there to grow your
> inner muscles.*

HANADI ALQATARI

Be proud of your strength. Even after going through every kind of trouble, you have to take on the challenge and let yourself grow into the strongest character.

Give yourself credit for all the strength you have inside yourself, no matter how broken, lost and confused you may feel. No matter what happens, just hold on to yourself. You must exercise that ability to make it stronger.

Let go of what you cannot change; focus on your strength. Nothing will be impossible for you if you never stop giving your best.

Life will always continue to go on, but use your inner power to heal all wounds.

> *Be your true self.*
> *Be who you are.*
> *Let go of all of the stories, labels*
> *and judgments.*
> *And the right people will love*
> *the real you.*

HANADI ALQATARI

You are best at being yourself. Sometimes when you watch small children you will see how free they are; they are their true natures, and they do not care what others think of them.

See the little child inside you. Play, have fun, enjoy the moment and do not worry about being judged.

This is the key to allowing your real self to shine today and every day.

Always make time to help others even when you are struggling with your own problems and end your day with a grateful heart. Every heart has the power to do this.

HANADI ALQATARI

It is a natural desire to help those we love in need. Helping others can be done each and every day. Just think about how you can spread love, hope, faith or motivation to others today. It is important to understand that helping others can actually help you and you will often feel better about yourself.

The next time the beloved people in your life are struggling with problems or need to make decisions, give them the same help and support you have received from others.

'

All that we are is the result of what we have thought.

BUDDHA

What you think, you become. Be aware that a single negative thought can destroy everything. Negative thought can seem easier than positive thought, because optimism and positivity need a lot of mental effort, but in return optimistic and positive people are happier, stronger and healthier, and enjoy more success than those who think negatively.

So . . . do you have the ability to determine your thoughts?

> *Most of us go through hard times. Let us be kind to one another.*

HANADI ALQATARI

Some people may have exactly your pain, some people have more than you, but in the end we can only control our actions in this life.

We all want to feel good and happy at all times, but in thinking about this I have come to the deep understanding that it is impossible. What is possible is asking for help. You are a person in need and so are all those around you.

It is okay to ask for support from others. People need other people.

'

Black, white, short, tall, fat, skinny, rich or poor. We are all equal.

HANADI ALQATARI

Our differences make the world beautiful. Some are smarter, some look better, some have different experiences, different abilities. But we all have equal rights to happiness, the equal right to succeed as human beings.

Help to spread respect in your community.

Just remember to be nice to everyone. We are all part of the same community and we can learn a lot from our differences.

*You are stronger than you
seem, smarter than you think.
Do not let your hard times
make you hate. There is
always hope.*

In our tough times there are always simple ways to deal well with them. Keep working hard to exercise your emotional strength; focus on what you have and appreciate what is around you. Be wise enough to understand that pain is a part of life; it helps us improve our control of every emotion.

When you are thankful and find strength in self-control, you have no reason to hate your situation.

'

What you think, you become.

HANADI ALQATARI

Be as conscious of your thoughts as you can be. When you are in control of them, you will know how simple it is to make things possible.

You are the leader of every single thought in your mind. When you need to overcome negative thinking, write down what you have been thinking negatively about in order to think more clearly.

Thinking positively will help you get in touch with your emotions and give you more control over the negative side of things.

Who are you, really? The answer is in your head.

'

Surround yourself with beautiful minds. Do not let someone's bad mood spoil your day.

HANADI ALQATARI

There are people whose positivity can keep you in the positive zone.

Minimise your contact with negative minds. Protect your positive energy by not participating in any drama they are trying to create.

Regardless of people who struggle to find a positive way of living, you can face each day with high spirit. Invest your time in people who know how to lift their own spirit.

Once you choose to surround yourself with beautiful minds, you clear away the negativity and allow yourself to create your own happiness.

'

Stop being a victim. Take charge of yourself and start creating your life.

HANADI ALQATARI

There will be times when we feel sad and start to play the victim with everything we've been through. That is our problem. We remain stuck in the past when we complain and feel sorry for ourselves.

So many of us avoid personal responsibility when things go wrong and blame everybody else, but the fact is that we have victimised ourselves.

However you are feeling today, know that it is your choice to let your past experiences teach you. Empower yourself with 'I can' and 'I will' statements.

Stop blaming and complaining. Take the step to begin looking at yourself and taking responsibility for your life.

'

Do not give up easily.
Keep learning how to do
it better next time.

HANADI ALQATARI

Every hard experience we go through can help teach us how to achieve success.

Whatever happens in your life, each failure teaches you something about yourself.

If you feel you are not good enough, try something different. Do not let that feeling bring you down, because you are learning. The experience you gain will help you achieve whatever you set out to achieve.

Are you doing something over and over again in different ways? Keep trying and be an inspiration to others by refusing to give up.

'

I am strong enough to fight to survive, because I am alive.

HANADI ALQATARI

You have the freedom to wake up every day and decide to step into the future with a brand new vision.

If you find yourself in a situation where nothing seems to be going right or you do not get something you wanted, we all have days like that; it is not your fault. Whatever bad things have appeared in your life, make sure that you can face your problems and stay strong for yourself.

Just believe in yourself and remember you are the only one who can survive your hard times. This means going through hardships and deciding not to surrender.

Your struggles rebuild your power. This is the time to begin gaining control over your future. That is strength.

'If you move on from the past hurt, you will continue to grow.

HANADI ALQATARI

To be strong you have to learn how to let the past hurt go. In my view that kind of emotional pain is a choice, focusing on the past pain rather than welcoming joy back into your life.

This moment, right now, speak to your mind and say you did not do anything to deserve being hurt. Remember that it is easy to release the pain. You just need to remind yourself of your ability to move beyond the pain you've experienced.

'

You cannot control everything in your life, but remember your reactions and attitude are your choice.

HANADI ALQATARI

Sometimes, when thinking of what has happened, you feel hopeless and believe you have no control. In that moment you just need to remind yourself you do have the power to decide how you respond.

Ask yourself how you are living your life. What do you want to achieve? You make so many decisions all the time, and the result of each one is either net positive or net negative. The more net positive decisions you can make, the more chances you will have to step closer to your goals.

Today take conscious control of all your decisions. You have the power and the choice to deal with the stuff you cannot control.

'

Start to do something, even if you do not know what you want to do. Find ways to explore what makes you feel energised and happy, no matter how small you start.

HANADI ALQATARI

What can you do today to create something you want in your life?

How do you learn to focus on those things that make you happy, that make you feel right in your heart?

Many people want to do something creative and achieve success in life. If that is exactly the kind of recognition you are looking for but you have no idea where to start, you just need to think about what matters to you. Pay attention to what makes you feel excited. If you explore with an open mind and trust in your own power to find excitement in doing new things in your life, your life will never be the same again.

No matter how little things may seem, be persistent. Every day is the starting point of doing something you want. Have a closer look at what you really want and motivate yourself to start right now.

'

Forgiving someone who wrogned us is not a weakness; it is a strong response.

HANADI ALQATARI

It is normal to feel it is hard to forgive and forget what someone did to you. Forgiveness is not a natural human response, but it is a choice that gives you strength, heart and a kind of peace.

Forgiveness does not mean denying the other person's responsibility for what they did to you, and it does not change that person.

Forgiveness empowers us and allows us to become a source of peace.

Free your soul and let go of the past with an open heart.

'*Beauty is feeling good about yourself; you do not need to be accepted by others. Confidence comes from being yourself.*

HANADI ALQATARI

Stand up for yourself with the confidence you were born with. Stand up for what you want to do, and what you want to be.

Learn who you are and believe in your capabilities. This is the key that should lead you where you want to go in this life. Do not worry if you are not confident in what you can do now. Remember confidence was your original nature before time started taking away.

No matter where you are now, where do you start? Find what gives you comfort within. When you find that comfort, your confidence will naturally build as a result.

'*Walking away does not mean you are not strong enough or wise enough. All the experiences and lessons are there to teach you what you need to know, so keep moving forward.*

HANADI ALQATARI

Everyone has been tested and felt the pain of learning lessons.

It is a huge waste of energy and emotions to stay with someone who lets you down or someone who is hard to love. You just have to walk away from the things that hurt you. Life is not easy, but you can start over, stop the cycle and let your heart heal so you can find who makes you feel wonderful. Surround yourself with loving relationships. Keep working on yourself and your recovery.

Something beautiful is out there waiting for you, if you have the courage to walk away and build yourself up emotionally.

'

Share your story. Tell the world how you got through your struggles. You can shine a light for others.

HANADI ALQATARI

We hide our failures and our fears, and sometimes we pretend everything is going great. That's why it takes courage to open up to others and share our story. Fear, struggles or other moments of weakness are things we all experience. No matter how large or small your story of struggle, feel free to tell stories of your hard times to your loved ones. Opening up about your life will surprise you with how much strength you have inside you.

Be honest and open with your loved ones about the good and bad. Find the beauty in being courageous by sharing your story. It will help others to know that they are not alone with their own stories.

Believe that how you got through situations can make a difference in the world and inspire others.

'

Building good habits starts with doing something once or twice.

HANADI ALQATARI

You might think that you are the type of person who does not like starting new habits and sticking to them, or you may feel that building new habits can be tough. Building good habits means thinking or doing the things you believe can improve your life every day. If a habit is positive, then you'll want to repeat it the next time. We do the best we can in life and sometimes we all just need a simple good practice on which to build change.

Developing good habits requires self-discipline, but self-discipline is also something you can develop. Choose one goal, think about the habit you will need and start working towards developing it, doing a little every day.

Breaking bad habits and creating permanent good habits will bring about change one step at a time and help you to achieve your dreams.

'

*Never forget that you have
the magic inside you.*

HANADI ALQATARI

The trick to believing in yourself is finding the magic that will drive you towards every one of your dreams. You carry all the power you need inside you. When you look in the mirror, you see your own image, but you cannot see the real you hidden inside. Whatever you are feeling and thinking, your inner magic will allow you to know yourself.

Open your heart and mind to know who you really are and how to work magic inside yourself.

*Once you know your worth,
you will learn how to receive
the abundance that the
world holds for you.*

HANADI ALQATARI

Feeling worthy of any blessing you may receive will help you find peace, knowing that you are perfect just as you are. To attract your heart's desires, you must know that everything you need is within you.

You may not be talented, but keep reminding yourself that you are worthy. Whatever you feel, remember life is just testing you. Instead of getting down on yourself and losing your sense of worth, you should hold your head up high and remember you deserve good things. If you keep this attitude of faith, you will feel worthy of all the good things life has to offer you and be able to live your life to its fullest potential.

'*It is not selfish to be primarily interested in your own goals.*

HANADI ALQATARI

Every day brings new opportunities to grow, and it is good to have plans and dreams. There is no point in worrying that your own happiness is selfish. Keep an open mind and think: what makes you happy? Are you the person you want to be right now? What can you do to achieve your dreams?

Dreams do not come if you spend hours on end waiting for them to happen. You should have enough selfishness to move on and follow your dreams. 'Good' selfishness is not bringing others down or using them to serve you, but it is the art of choosing your own beliefs, your own priorities and your own opinion about yourself instead of allowing other people to define who you are.

Do what is best for you, be the best person you can be, and make others happy. That is the key to living a successful life.

'

It is not about finding the time to get things done; it is how you find the motivation to start doing things that truly inspire you every day.

HANADI ALQATARI

What matters most is to keep working for yourself, keep motivating yourself to do the things you truly want to do. Think about what you should do for yourself that you can work on today. How much time you have does not matter; it is about finding the motivation to get things done. No matter how fast you go, the goal is to be closer to a meaningful achievement.

'No matter how high you have climbed, you still need to hear the right words to believe in those great things that you have worked to achieve.

HANADI ALQATARI

Our belief in ourselves helps us become successful. Even if this feeling comes from within, sometimes people say words that spark your heart, or put your imagination in over-drive, or that simply build your self-confidence and inspire you to try to succeed even more.

We all need to hear something to lift our spirits, whether going through difficult times or achieving positive change.

'

Overthinking leads to negative emotions and sadness.

HANADI ALQATARI

Sometimes it is easy to become stuck in negativity and start overthinking when something goes wrong. Overthinking is an easy habit to fall into when we have no control over an aspect of life.

I encourage you to think more positively about every single thing you already have and accept as a normal part of your life, instead of overthinking and asking yourself why you are not getting what you deserve. Do not focus on what is wrong with life, do not let the action of others influence your emotions and do not let circumstances dictate your mood.

Allow yourself to think creatively, adjust your dreams to reality and never stop dreaming.

'

Some experiences leave us
feeling weak and helpless.
Never give up; you have the
courage to decide that you
are strong.

HANADI ALQATARI

As you grow, the way you look at hard times will change. When hard times hit and the challenges you face are great, you can use your sadness as a source of growth and learn how strong you are. We need to feel pain to wake ourselves up and feel alive.

Fight hard to shine the light of your strength, beat fear if you face it and inspire others to live their lives by showing them the courage you have. But remember that courage does not mean you do not get afraid; it is about deciding to take action despite your fear and finding how much stronger you become by learning from your experience as you go.

The next time you feel weak and helpless, do not let fear stop you from moving forward with your life. It is your chance to practise being stronger.

‘

A smart woman finds strength in kindness to make a difference.

HANADI ALQATARI

Kindness is so important. I believe that a simple act of kindness can change someone's life in a really big way. Create positive energy in any way you can, spread good vibrations by being kind, and hopefully you will inspire others to do the same.

Some unkind people need your kindness. By choosing to respond with positivity to these people, you can build positive relationships and inspire them to show kindness in turn.

Remember that an act of kindness does not have to cost a thing. Being kind to others will make you respect yourself for doing something great and give you a sense of purpose.

'

Forgiveness is so hard sometimes, but it frees your mental and emotional energies so that you can apply them to moving forward for the better.

HANADI ALQATARI

Forgiveness will improve all your relationships and help you to go on stronger and happier.

Forgiveness is never easy, especially when others hurt us. But I believe that, if we are feeling pain, it is better to forgive than to take any action that may create greater pain. We all have a choice to spend energy creating peace in our heart and an amazing future for ourselves, rather than spending it trying to hang on to contempt and get revenge on others.

Remind yourself that the most powerful and greatest emotion, after love, is forgiveness. Fill your heart with it. It does not mean you approve what happened, but it means that you are strong enough to move on with your life.

‘

Do not be a lioness hunting for the kill.

UNKNOWN

We are not all born with inner strength, but inside us we have everything we need to develop our inner strength.

Your inner strength is measured by how you use it to find the internal courage to keep going, regardless of the challenges you may be facing. Sometimes you may feel it is difficult to find gentle strength, especially when you have to respond to things you do not have control over. Whenever you feel that, remember controlling your emotions is a kind of inner strength that will make you happier with yourself and a stronger person on the outside too.

'

Do not allow anyone to make you feel discouraged or unworthy. If you do not believe in yourself, nobody else will.

HANADI ALQATARI

Sometimes you will get into an argument with someone who will try to bring you down. Negative people will actually feed off your energy, and this will give them more power to tell you you cannot live your dream while leaving you feeling drained. If you allow yourself to be controlled by the opinions of others, you will spend your life living according to their rules.

Highly successful people withdraw from negativity. They do not need to prove they are right. Doing so doesn't make you weak.

Always ask yourself, 'Do I want to conform to what others think or do I want to live happily?'

If you know exactly what you want and start doing it today, you will spread positive vibes that will be reflected back to you.

'

Accept and respect other people's differences.

HANADI ALQATARI

We can always learn from our differences. They help us to learn more about the world, to learn more about ourselves and to grow spiritually. Everyone thinks they are right and wants to explain their viewpoint and opinions. Be open to others and take time to listen to their opinions. You do not have to accept their opinions, but you have to respect their right to share their thoughts.

Listen and learn from everyone, and do not be afraid to express your own viewpoint, whether you agree or disagree. They say that everyone we meet can teach us something new. You do not need to convince others that you are right or be persuaded that they are right; it's all about being different from each other but accepted and respected. Always focus on the opinion, not the person. You might get a spark of inspiration from someone who has different experiences from you.

‘

Free yourself from the fear of social judgment.

HANADI ALQATARI

There are always many sides to a story. Sometimes we only have part of the story, sometimes we have the whole story and sometimes we have the story wrong. Ask yourself, 'Why am I judging this person?' Every time you judge someone else, you will be judged in the same way. Think twice before you judge someone.

Stop perpetuating the cycle of judgment by replacing judgment with giving space to others to be who they are. At the same time, be who you need to be. Find the part of yourself that you dislike the most and start to accept it. Do not try to impress others or worry about what others think of you.

Focusing on the good in your life and spending more time on things that really matter will bring peace to you and to the world.

The less you judge others, the less you will be judged by others.

'

The struggles in our lives may be difficult, but each challenge that comes our way offers us a path to find the strength that we have within.

HANADI ALQATARI

Never give up. You always have a chance to rise above the challenges and train yourself to learn by embracing your struggles. When things do not go your way, do not let the pain of your situation make you feel hopeless. Dealing with a challenging time is a hard thing to do, but you have to work hard to strengthen your inner power, like your muscles burning towards the end of the run.

'*Keep going and take a risk when you feel like giving up.*

HANADI ALQATARI

Sometimes in life we feel lost and we just want to give up, especially when we are worrying about what we cannot control. Many of our worries are about negative things that have not even occurred in our lives.

Keep going. Do not give up. Focus on what you can create today. Keep making mistakes and trying again; making mistakes means you are doing something in your life and learning from it.

Do not delay your happiness by telling yourself that you are not able to move towards something you have always wanted to do.

Now, think about it and make it happen.

'

Do not be afraid to express yourself.

HANADI ALQATARI

We all struggle with free self-expression and wish that we had more courage to speak up and express ourselves clearly. We all want to do our best. I know exactly what it is like to feel afraid to speak up and get what you want and deserve. We would love the confidence to show ourselves to the world. Our great challenge is being ourselves.

Fear steals our freedom to be creative in expressing our true selves. Fear leaves everyone powerless and ready to give up. Fear allows others to hurt us because we do not speak up for ourselves.

When you have difficulty with self-expression, do not choose to sit alone in your room, feeling powerless and broken down. From now, remember you always have the chance to speak up for yourself and to be more courageous.

The more you express yourself, the more motivated you are to follow your dreams.

'
If you fall over, just get back up again.

HANADI ALQATARI

It does not matter how many failures you experience; it does not matter how long you have been struggling with problems in your life. Whether it is at work, at home or in any area of your life, it is hard not to get tired of failure and it is easy to quit trying. But if you believe in yourself enough and if you want success in your life, get back up again with confidence. It is not over until you win.

Remember, every time you fail and fall, you gain strength, courage, hope and the confidence to get back up.

You were born to win and shine and there is always a way to pick yourself up again.

'

Do you act like someone else in order to please everyone around you?

HANADI ALQATARI

If you follow others without thinking of what you want, because you want everyone to like you, then you will be trapped in the way you live your life, a slave to the opinions of others. It is important to make your own choices. Learn how to protect your desires and dreams while staying open to only the inspired opinions of others.

You can open your heart to all around you without being a people-pleaser. Always believe in yourself as the controller of your own dreams and goals.

Stop trying to please everyone and focus on just one person: you.

'

Choose to focus on what really matters in your life in order to move yourself closer to your hopes, dreams and goals.

HANADI ALQATARI

If you spend most of your time worrying and doing things that keep you very busy, consider whether you are spending so much time working on 'urgent' things that you aren't spending enough time on things that are really important to you.

Whatever urgent things you are struggling with, seek out what will make you feel real fulfilment.

'

Protect your positive space
against negative influences
by talking about positive
daily events.

HANADI ALQATARI

Are you surrounding yourself with people who behave negatively? Are you surrounding yourself with people who poison your spirit and involve you in drama? Are you allowing yourself to be hurt by letting haters into your life?

Think about negative people who are poisoning your thoughts, controlling your behaviour and limiting your actions and opportunities. Who are these people and why are they in your life?

Remember what they do and who they are, then tell them that they must either leave or adjust their attitude and be more supportive and kinder. At the same time, you must surround yourself with positive, inspiring people who will reflect the person you want to be. Ask them to come into your circles, to brighten your life simply by being in it.

'

Do not always wait for a better condition or a better time to do whatever you want to do. Life is happening now.

HANADI ALQATARI

Each day and every moment of our lives has surprises, challenges or unknowns. The simplest way to live is to do what we should do, not making excuses or holding off until a better time. The world opens up unforeseen resources when we take our chance to live and love. Do what you plan to do. The perfect time may never exist if you keep postponing things for the right time, rather than doing them. Who knows if the right moment will come or not?

Of course there is always another chance, but life is too short to be wasted on waiting for the right time to get moving.

Remember you have all the energy and the strength to do anything right now.

*Choose to do what will make
your soul happy and fly, or stop
hating what you are doing.*

HANADI ALQATARI

You always have the choice, the power, the courage and the opportunity to take yourself out of any position that cannot open your heart, your mind and your spirit to feel fulfilment and inner peace.

You hate your job? Find another job, quit, start your own business, or change your thoughts and start loving your job.

You hate your children's school? Take the step of talking to the school in order to come up with some solutions, or perhaps it is time to find another arrangement for your little ones.

You dislike your friends' attitude? Figure out the problem and learn how to adjust their attitude if you can, or reduce the time you spend hanging out with them. If you cannot stand being alone, look for better people.

You hate your life? Change it by choosing to live freely in each and every moment, and began to build a new life by moving yourself away from anything you hate.

Try to get out of your ingrained ways and move ahead until you love your life.

> *'While you are working on your dreams, plan to achieve them. Be sure to enjoy the trip and be proud of every step you take.*
>
> HANADI ALQATARI

However you are working towards your dreams each day, give yourself time to enjoy all the steps that you take, no matter how small they are.

You have to work hard towards your dreams. Some dreams take years and a huge amount of energy to achieve. So it is important to enjoy working towards them.

For example, you set a goal of losing weight. You will need to work out and make a plan, but remind yourself to enjoy the challenge with all your heart.

'

There will be some people who will not like the way you live your own life.

HANADI ALQATARI

What happens when you learn to say *no*? It sounds simple enough. Surely you are not the only one taking responsibility for your own life and not following the same path as others. Over time others will come to understand, will respect you and will leave you alone.

Do not let the wrong people scratch off your dreams. While you are out there following your dream, living life in your own way and getting closer and closer to the life you want, know that there will be some people who will not like your free will and they will try to guilt you. Do not worry about others. Do not let them get to you. Decide today to create and design your own life in the way you love.

You are strong enough to live your life in your own way, not like everyone else.

'*No matter how much you try, no matter how nice you are, there will always be people who do not like your free will, your independence and the way you live your life.*

HANADI ALQATARI

We all have different opinions on how to live our lives, so we must decide to take actions without the approval of others.

When it is your loved ones calling your actions or struggles crazy, artfully deal with them. Lovingly explain that you need your freedom. Being nice to those we love is right and giving attention to those close to us is good, but never at the cost of our freedom.

Nothing in life is fixed, so you must find a way to let go of your desire to control what others think is right for you.

You have no idea how much freedom comes with feeling that your life is fully yours. Just start to have the courage to live in your own ways.

'

Keep your cool and maintain self-control when responding to others' aggression.

HANADI ALQATARI

We often encounter people who are aggressive, judgmental or rude, whether they be an angry driver, pushy relative or aggressive supervisor.

There are many books on how to handle aggressive and controlling people. But, simply put, one of the most basic ways to deal with aggression is to keep your cool.

There are times we feel we are stuck with a very difficult friend, manager or partner. We have the right to be treated with respect, and some people do not respect this right. But you have the power to concentrate your energy on self-control.

Keep in mind, if you allow your anger to control every reaction, it will become a habit.

*Live every second of your life
with the energy of hope,
strength and love.*

*Our great goal in life is to live
at the level of hope, strength
and love, to shape our inner
world and our outer reality
and reach the deepest level
of ourselves.*

*You deserve to be free and
happy.*

Celebrate and move on.

Lightning Source UK Ltd.
Milton Keynes UK
UKHW010850141218
333983UK00004B/93/P

9 781789 630077